13 Weeks To Recover The Real You.

~ A Workbook for the Burnt Out.

Unearth Your Shadow.
Learn to Find & Love the Whole You. Practice
Self-care & Self-responsibility as Virtues.

Wren Síofra Lloyd

Dedication

For Ivan
Whose unconditional acceptance
taught me that all of me is wanted &
needed, right here, right now!

Lies

Let your lies lay intimately,
Fearlessly naked beside the truth.
Let them stare into each other
with compassion and acceptance.
Let truth be the strong but silent type.

Let your lies reach out,
Safely touch the truth.
Explore the truth,
Without judgment.
Knowing truth knows them
And sees their heart.

Let each lie see itself.
And see from what it hid.
Let them melt and join with the truth
Until they become truth together.
Let them join and transform,
Joyous to transcend fear.

Let them not be ashamed
Of their past.
Let them be loved
For their innocence.
Let them be remembered lovingly
For their willingness to be seen.

~ Wren Síofra Lloyd

About The Author

Wren Síofra ('she-frah) Lloyd is a homeopath, painter, poet and mother to 4.
In this workbook, she brings together powerful learning and discoveries made in the process of working with patients, healing her complex trauma (through somatic experiencing and breathwork), and working to overcome her martyr tendencies.
If you are interested in The Enneagram, as a child she developed the strategies of number 2, wing 3 ... so she has first hand knowledge of being "The Helper" and of the shadowy, subconscious agendas of the martyr archetype.

How To Use This Workbook.

- Read the orientation chapter below and any text as you go through.
- Don't skip any reading if you want to experience the magical process.
- Do your workbook workouts first thing in the morning, before anything else!
- Wake up 20 minutes early, if needs be, because it may save your day! Let people know the importance of what you're doing & that you need space.
- It is important to write with the intention of getting to know your fears, your resentment and your sense of obligation and particularly of breathing them out with the intention of letting them go.
- If you feel the need in any of the sections to write more and let more go, go to the extension pages at the back until you feel complete!
- Take your time and do the work regularly. You are changing the conditioning and habits of a lifetime and that takes self-responsibility and commitment.
- Use the evaluation page at the end of every week. By evaluating we become conscious of the value of our work, including the subtle accumulative changes we may otherwise miss.
- Set the intention to gradually open up and be honest with yourself.
- If shame arises, use creative imagination: Imagine you reach into the small child within you, put an arm around them and remind them that, without exception, all human beings have a full set of the human traits & feelings, and they are all essential in some way.
- Start to offer yourself love and acceptance, whatever arises, and remind yourself that all blame is off track and you don't have to try to defend yourself.
- Give this to yourself.

Orientation:

There will never be a better time for self-care, however long you try to postpone it.
There never was a more instinctive, rightful & essential activity than self-care.
The most honest, respectful and grown-up thing you can do is meet your needs
before deciding if you really want to help with the needs of others!

Surprised? This likely isn't what you were taught as a child.

Were You Groomed into The Order of The Martyr?

It's pretty standard practice to expect to gain love & avoid punishment if you please
others:

- By meeting their needs [for quiet, obedience, love, lies, your stuff],
- By foregoing your needs [not being 'a nuisance'],
- By avoiding any behaviour they have chosen to label 'bad'.

Did it teach you to be 'good' & 'kind', as they intended?
No! Because, what they asked for is unnatural. Maybe you started to lie:

- To lie about yourself to appear 'virtuous' & avoid feeling shame.
- To people-please to get what you want & avoid what you don't want,
- To see yourself as a powerless victim because you took on the shame & felt forced.
- To secretly judge others the way you felt judged.
- To compete to be "better" ~ the most selfless, perfect, worthy, lovable, long-suffering person - to resolve the shame you felt about your hidden, true nature.
- To hide your true nature ~ your needs, desires & the parts of you which others deemed 'bad' ... [usually the juicy, awesome bits!]
- To hide the things you didn't want to share,
- To Lie To Yourself about yourself and to lose yourself in the process!

✸ You divorced and denied the parts of yourself that you concluded were
'unacceptable' ... & those parts became your 'shadow'. We all did it. We all have
shadows.

You learned from unconscious martyrs & manipulators, who learned from unconscious martyrs & manipulators, that you mustn't be selfish and you must hide your 'unacceptable' needs, desires, thoughts and feelings.

You also learned that only martyrs & their suffering are righteous.
Your parents and elders made you aware of their righteousness by showing how they suffered on your behalf.
You were made to pay for your basic care, in obedience and love and lies and stuff.

You're probably knee deep in passing this to your kids right now, so it's good you stopped by.

You Contain All Human Traits

"All of you is wanted and needed, right here, right now."

All human traits are essential so have always existed in all humans.
Every trait is trying to meet a real need.
Knowing this, you can accept your shadow traits as 'normal' and 'universal'.
All traits can be expressed in more constructive and less constructive ways.
We express all our traits, externally or internally, to some extent, every day.
If you don't recognise a trait in yourself, you'll find it in your shadow.

✴ You reduce your ability to choose how a trait is expressed when you deny it and put it in your shadow. Accept all traits lovingly, respect the needs they represent and they can be constructive.

Someone says "You're greedy!"
You think "We have all traits, so that has to be somewhat true."
When you offer yourself acceptance, shame can no longer reign.

✴ When you no longer create shame or defend yourself against shame by labelling others 'bad', the desire to fight leaves, and you step out of victimhood, right into the loving arms of your personal power.

Take The Human Emotion Anger ...

All emotions are triggered by thoughts. Thoughts are instantaneous and often unconscious. Anger is an instinctive response to the thought – "I'm powerless". Anger is needed to protect boundaries and get you out of tight spaces. You were born knowing how to do it! It has been essential to humans for eternity.

Most parents didn't learn how to express their anger constructively or deal with their child's anger & maybe the child's anger didn't suit the parent's needs. Your parents probably didn't teach you to express your anger constructively. Instead, they made it 'bad', whilst they lived a double standard because they couldn't manage their own anger.
To avoid punishment you swallowed anger and convinced yourself you were 'powerless' and 'powerful' parents could operate double standards. Suppressing your emotions makes you feel heavy, emotionless and weak. Do it long enough and you'll feel a kind of 'dead and heavy' called "depression".

Depression

If you have depression, most likely you have a lake of suppressed anger. Depression is a shadow sickness. You're depressed because you believe you are powerless to change things, longterm. "I'll be shamed & powerless if I try."

Powerlessness

Whilst you might identify as a powerless victim, every human has a potential for devastating power! Every day you have the power to end another's life, which you choose not to use. You even had this as a child!
You need power to take action in life, but often you choose to give up power in order to avoid shame. *You disempower yourself* to keep hiding from your shadow.

But shame can't co-exist with self acceptance.
And depression lifts when you express your feelings and stop neutering your power.

Since you're actually all powerful and you are choosing not to use your power, you must recognise your responsibility for your own suffering when you do things that are not right for you and when you sacrifice your needs to meet the needs of others.

The Rewards of Martyrdom

The martyr is a *victim* archetype. When we unconsciously play the martyr, we don't sacrifice ourselves without expecting payback! In fact, we make our needs the responsibility of others, expecting others to 'justly' reward us for our 'sacrifice and hard work'. [Send yourself a little love if you recognise this.]
When people don't notice or understand the unspoken deal, our expectations are not met and we label others 'bad' and ourselves 'neglected', 'better-than', 'good', etc.
We behave as if we are powerless, but in fact, we:

- Live a falsely "virtuous life" ~ Collect a Self-righteousness Token.
- Become 'important' by sacrificing our needs and knowing the needs of others they didn't even know they had! ~ Collect a Self-righteousness Token.
- Ensure people stay with us, due to the co-dependency we encourage, & 'you owe me' ~ Collect a Self-righteousness Token.
- Become self-righteousness to inflate our opinion of our own contribution & 'now the whole world needs us and owes us'! ~ Collect another Self-righteousness Token.
- Get to feel 'better than others' because they don't take care of us with equal self-sacrifice and knowledge of our needs ~ Collect another Self-righteousness Token.
- Finally break from self-neglect. Others do take care of us then, but our shadow plays the victim - punishing the abuser with "It's about time you did something for me after all I've sacrificed for you!". ~ Collect yet another Self-righteousness Token.

... and round and round we go.

If you're a martyr, some of your acts will be altruistic, nothing is ever all-or-nothing. But if your needs were suppressed & you made that mean "my needs are wrong and I'm not important", now you are probably gathering self-righteousness tokens and self importance to resolve your sense of worthlessness. And you'll hide your 'unacceptable' self-righteous thoughts as subconscious shadow chatter.

Monitor your inner dialogue and you'll hear your self-esteem issues, your judgments, and your resentment fuelling your subconscious [and thus inevitably your actions] all day long. *It's happening to all of us. It's human.*

By reclaiming and accepting your shadow you can begin to choose your thoughts, feelings and behaviour more reliably. The babble will continue in the background but you will hear it and be able to choose your actions regardless.

Get To Know Your Shadow

Your shadow may contain:
- Hidden needs & desires ~ a lot of what you love!
- Personal power ~ your "Yes!", your "No!"
- Self-love & self-care.
- Self-responsibility.
- Self-preservation instincts.
- Your Real Life Path &
- Much of your Creative Energy!

You can't hide your shadow if it is hidden from yourself! Yikes!
At the reins of your subconscious all day, it has a knack of leaving a mark that everyone can see apart from you! So your friends and family know your shadow better than you know it and they love you anyway.

There's not that much agreement about what's 'bad'. You may have put 'being nice to people' in your shadow if it was considered 'creepy' by your elders. Your partner has a whole bunch of different 'bad' in their shadow, and some of those things may be what makes them attractive. How funny that we are busy, years after we grow up, still trying to hide these things and hide from them, rather than listening to our own opinion! It's time to be the sovereign in your own life now.

Take a Step Into Integrity

Your first responsibility as an adult is to maintain your physical and mental well-being as you would maintain your house. It's your house. No one else lives there.
If you don't maintain your house, you & others may be forced to invest a whole lot more in putting you back together.
You'll find a section in your Daily Workout that prompts you to begin to develop work-arounds for some of the services you don't authentically want to carry out for others or yourself!

Be gentle with your family and friends & give them plenty of time to adjust. Their adjustment will lag behind yours because theirs grows out of seeing yours in action. You've raised your children, and encouraged others, to expect the sort of selfless care you offered. That's what 'love' has looked like up until now. You set the standards. Add new ways to express love and gradually find loving work-arounds for services you don't want to provide.

Be especially gentle with your children because they've known no different, and you've taught them that a 'good' parent sacrifices themselves. Let the culture change little by little, so they don't feel abandoned and begin to see themselves as victims. Speak openly about what you've discovered and make small changes.

Encourage your children to express and gradually meet their own needs, as appropriate to their age and ability and model this for them with your own actions. If you have a partner, offer respect to their needs by expecting them to put their own needs first too.

Step out of the toxic culture of martyrdom & grow a new culture in your family. Break the cycle.

But How Do I know When to Help Others?

It's not your responsibility to meet the needs of others. Respect them as powerful creators & give them space to meet their own needs or learn to meet their own needs. Don't give others responsibility for your needs - they'll do a disappointing job compared to you because you know exactly how you like it & you're now free to meet your own needs. Stand on your strong two feet, straighten your back, raise your chin and step into your personal power. Lead by example and wait for your loved ones to join in.

There's an exception or two.

You have a parental duty to meet the needs of your children until they can meet them themselves. Observe carefully and when you know they are ready [usually they'll ask], gradually hand over more autonomy to them, whilst offering them a safe harbour to return to if it feels too much. They'll gain self esteem from being able to meet their own needs, if they are not pushed.

Different children reach independence in different ways at vastly different stages, so try to trust the needs they express, thereby you encourage them to trust themselves too. If you're reluctant to fulfil one of their needs, find a work-around which works for you all.

You can choose to help anyone, but watch out! You've got a lot of conditioning to overcome! When your own cup is thoroughly topped up with reserves & you've gained enough awareness of your shadow, you might enjoy offering help to others with what overflows your cup. A "No thanks" might initially hurt your ego if helping previously made you feel worthy. Improve your sense of worth by using the time to look after yourself instead.

Be sure to check in with your heart before you offer help or say "yes" to a request for help. See below:

How To Reach Your Heart

It is strangely easy. Indeed, do it before you make any decision!
You only need what your body already has and already knows!
You just need to tap into it.
You can do it anywhere, anytime ... and you won't even look strange ....
- Take space to think first.
- Breathe deeply.
- Feel your feet on the ground.
- Feel your fingers in your palms.

Continue breathing deeply until you feel you are totally in your body [it could take 20 seconds or a minute] ... then silently ask your heart the question and you'll hear a quiet voice from inside, which feels weirdly certain.
You're a recovering approval addict so only a resounding heart's "Yes!" Counts.
If that "yes" doesn't arrive don't betray yourself.
You are in the business of teaching your body to trust that you'll listen.
Find a work-around.

Now, go retrieve your life! Your Daily Workouts begin.

Awake

If you've lost sight
Of what you're here for.
If you've lost sight
Of what you are!
Remember that being human
Is creation and expression,
For its own, pure sake.
Everything good comes
From that place.

If you've forgotten to create
And to express yourself
Openly, with vulnerability,
Fearlessly, like a child ...
Remember!
Cry! Love! Speak! Sing!
Whatever it takes ...
Awake.

~ Wren Síofra Lloyd

About The Daily Workouts

Daily Workout activities are designed to be combined with breath.
Breathe out fear and judgment. Breathe in self love.
Breathe to connect with your heart.

'I notice a fear that' ~
Daily, bring awareness to fears passing through. Release them by taking a deep
breath in through the nose and out with a big, soft sigh. Notice less stress and anxiety
as fears move through. They can only remain if you ignore them. They may turn up
daily, but persist and they will move through.

'I notice these judgments about others' ~
Let them out. Are they part of your martyrdom pattern?
If you live by this sword you die by this sword ... judging yourself just as harshly.
Breathe them out daily and relationships with yourself & others gradually feel
healthy.

'Two things about myself that I am affirming & accepting' ~
It takes practice to build new habits. Breathe in the affirmations and self love! Old
parts of you will try to intervene. Politely shut them down and repeat your
affirmation.

'One Way in which I've been playing the martyr' ~
Self examination leads to self awareness. See the ways you're playing martyr. Scribble
them in the margins! 9/10ths is awareness, the rest is a little time to integrate it.
"In reality I am": find your truth. You are powerful remember!

'Today I feel obliged to' ~
What's weighing on you?
Do you want, need or have to do these things? Reach Your Heart and find out. Breathe
out the feeling of obligation and the martyr resentment that arises.
My work-around: Delete, Delegate, Delay or Dominate ...

- Delete: Is the job yours or someone else's business? Maybe you can just say no?

- Delegate: Can someone else do that task? Offer it to a professional?

- Delay: Would you like to do it if it was a different day?

- Dominate: If you look at your martyr thoughts, can you check again? Can you explode those thoughts and then do the task with passion? Is there a way of getting it done that suits everyone? A third way? This takes imagination & practice. Persevere.

Today I Want & Need [for me] ~

Ahhhh. Saving the best for last. The best way to shed your martyr is to start meeting your needs ... better still .... your needs and desires. It may take a while to learn what you need and desire but your heart knows! Reach Your Heart [with breath], then give it to yourself - liberally!

My work-around ~ how are you going to make space, time and resources to give this to yourself today?

You are important. Look out for the martyr tendency of setting a boundary then dropping your boundary at the slightest pressure. It's not just about fear, it's also a martyr trick by which to gain self-righteousness tokens if you've felt powerless and rewarded yourself in this way in the past.

What do you *really* want instead?

Extension Pages & Note Pages

There are extension pages at the back of this workbook if you really feel the need to do more of any particular workout ... but don't burn yourself out, there's always more tomorrow.

You'll also find pages for your own notes.

Now You Can Start ...
13 Weeks To Recover
The Real You.

~ A Workbook for the Burnt Out.

Unearth Your Shadow.
Learn to Find & Love the Whole You. Practice Self-care &
Self-responsibility as Virtues.

My Daily Workout   Date.   /   /

I notice a fear that

* ....[Breathe it out]

* ....[Breathe it out]

* ....[Breathe it out]

* ....[Breathe it out]

* ....[Breathe it out]

I notice these judgments about others

* ....[Breathe it out]

* ....[Breathe it out]

Two things I'm accepting & affirming about myself

* ....

* ....

One Way in which I've been playing the martyr

* ....[Breathe it out]

In reality I am: ....

Today I feel obliged to

* ....[Breathe it out]

My work-around: ....

* ....[Breathe it out]

My work-around: ....

Today I Need [for me]

* ....

My work-around: ....

* ....

My work-around: ....

* ....

My work-around: ....

[Use the extension pages at the back of this workbook if you need to do more]

(c) Wren Síofra Lloyd

My Daily Workout   Date.   /   /

I notice a fear that

* ....[Breathe it out]
* ....[Breathe it out]
* ....[Breathe it out]
* ....[Breathe it out]
* ....[Breathe it out]

I notice these judgments about others

* ....[Breathe it out]
* ....[Breathe it out]

Two things I'm accepting & affirming about myself

* ....
* ....

One Way in which I've been playing the martyr

* ....[Breathe it out]

In reality I am: ....

Today I feel obliged to

* ....[Breathe it out]

My work-around: ....
* ....[Breathe it out]

My work-around: ....

Today I Need [for me]

* ....

My work-around: ....
* ....

My work-around: ....
* ....

My work-around: ....

[Use the extension pages at the back of this workbook if you need to do more]

(c) Wren Síofra Lloyd

My Daily Workout   Date.   /   /

I notice a fear that
* ....[Breathe it out]
* ....[Breathe it out]
* ....[Breathe it out]
* ....[Breathe it out]
* ....[Breathe it out]

I notice these judgments about others
* ....[Breathe it out]
* ....[Breathe it out]

Two things I'm accepting & affirming about myself
* ....
* ....

One Way in which I've been playing the martyr
* ....[Breathe it out]
In reality I am: ....

Today I feel obliged to
* ....[Breathe it out]
My work-around: ....
* ....[Breathe it out]
My work-around: ....

Today I Need [for me]
* ....
My work-around: ....
* ....
My work-around: ....
* ....
My work-around: ....

[Use the extension pages at the back of this workbook if you need to do more]

(c) Wren Síofra Lloyd

My Daily Workout   Date.   /   /

I notice a fear that

* ....[Breathe it out]

* ....[Breathe it out]

* ....[Breathe it out]

* ....[Breathe it out]

* ....[Breathe it out]

I notice these judgments about others

* ....[Breathe it out]

* ....[Breathe it out]

Two things I'm accepting & affirming about myself

* ....

* ....

One Way in which I've been playing the martyr

* ....[Breathe it out]

In reality I am: ....

Today I feel obliged to

* ....[Breathe it out]

My work-around: ....

* ....[Breathe it out]

My work-around: ....

Today I Need [for me]

* ....

My work-around: ....

* ....

My work-around: ....

* ....

My work-around: ....

[Use the extension pages at the back of this workbook if you need to do more]

(c) Wren Síofra Lloyd

My Daily Workout   Date.   /   /

I notice a fear that
* ....[Breathe it out]
* ....[Breathe it out]
* ....[Breathe it out]
* ....[Breathe it out]
* ....[Breathe it out]

I notice these judgments about others
* ....[Breathe it out]
* ....[Breathe it out]

Two things I'm accepting & affirming about myself
* ....
* ....
....

One Way in which I've been playing the martyr
* ....[Breathe it out]
In reality I am: ....

Today I feel obliged to
* ....[Breathe it out]
My work-around: ....
* ....[Breathe it out]
My work-around: ....

Today I Need [for me]
* ....
My work-around: ....
* ....
My work-around: ....
* ....
My work-around: ....

[Use the extension pages at the back of this workbook if you need to do more]

(c) Wren Síofra Lloyd

My Daily Workout   Date.   /   /

I notice a fear that

* ....[Breathe it out]
* ....[Breathe it out]
* ....[Breathe it out]
* ....[Breathe it out]
* ....[Breathe it out]

I notice these judgments about others

* ....[Breathe it out]
* ....[Breathe it out]

Two things I'm accepting & affirming about myself

* ....
* ....

One Way in which I've been playing the martyr

* ....[Breathe it out]

In reality I am: ....

Today I feel obliged to

* ....[Breathe it out]

My work-around: ....

* ....[Breathe it out]

My work-around: ....

Today I Need [for me]

* ....

My work-around: ....

* ....

My work-around: ....

* ....

My work-around: ....

[Use the extension pages at the back of this workbook if you need to do more]

(c) Wren Síofra Lloyd

My Daily Workout   Date.   /   /

I notice a fear that

* ....[Breathe it out]
* ....[Breathe it out]
* ....[Breathe it out]
* ....[Breathe it out]
* ....[Breathe it out]

I notice these judgments about others

* ....[Breathe it out]
* ....[Breathe it out]

Two things I'm accepting & affirming about myself

* ....
* ....

One Way in which I've been playing the martyr

* ....[Breathe it out]

In reality I am: ....

Today I feel obliged to

* ....[Breathe it out]

My work-around: ....
* ....[Breathe it out]

My work-around: ....

Today I Need [for me]

* ....

My work-around: ....
* ....

My work-around: ....
* ....

My work-around: ....

[Use the extension pages at the back of this workbook if you need to do more]

(c) Wren Síofra Lloyd

My Week

To Discover Value We Must Evaluate

"Be faithful to that which
exists within yourself."
~ André Gide

This week's anxiety score: out of 10 =

How does it compare to last week?

This week's 'shame' score: out of 10 =

How does to compare to last week?

What challenges did you overcome?

Did you begin to see any surprising changes?

My Daily Workout   Date.   /   /

I notice a fear that
* ....[Breathe it out]
* ....[Breathe it out]
* ....[Breathe it out]
  ....[Breathe it out]
* ....[Breathe it out]
* ....[Breathe it out]

I notice these judgments about others
* ....[Breathe it out]
* ....[Breathe it out]

Two things I'm accepting & affirming about myself
* ....
* ....
  ....

One Way in which I've been playing the martyr
* ....[Breathe it out]

In reality I am: ....

Today I feel obliged to
* ....[Breathe it out]

My work-around: ....
* ....[Breathe it out]

My work-around: ....

Today I Need [for me]
* ....

My work-around: ....
* ....

My work-around: ....
* ....

My work-around: ....

[Use the extension pages at the back of this workbook if you need to do more]

(c) Wren Síofra Lloyd

My Daily Workout

Date.   /   /

I notice a fear that

* ....[Breathe it out]
* ....[Breathe it out]
* ....[Breathe it out]
* ....[Breathe it out]
* ....[Breathe it out]

I notice these judgments about others

* ....[Breathe it out]
* ....[Breathe it out]

Two things I'm accepting & affirming about myself

* ....
* ....

One Way in which I've been playing the martyr

* ....[Breathe it out]

In reality I am: ....

Today I feel obliged to

* ....[Breathe it out]

My work-around: ....
* ....[Breathe it out]

My work-around: ....

Today I Need [for me]

* ....

My work-around: ....
* ....

My work-around: ....
* ....

My work-around: ....

[Use the extension pages at the back of this workbook if you need to do more]

(c) Wren Síofra Lloyd

My Daily Workout   Date.   /   /

I notice a fear that
* ....[Breathe it out]
* ....[Breathe it out]
* ....[Breathe it out]
* ....[Breathe it out]
* ....[Breathe it out]

I notice these judgments about others
* ....[Breathe it out]
* ....[Breathe it out]

Two things I'm accepting & affirming about myself
* ....
* ....

One Way in which I've been playing the martyr
* ....[Breathe it out]
In reality I am: ....

Today I feel obliged to
* ....[Breathe it out]
My work-around: ....
* ....[Breathe it out]
My work-around: ....

Today I Need [for me]
* ....
My work-around: ....
* ....
My work-around: ....
* ....
My work-around: ....

[Use the extension pages at the back of this workbook if you need to do more]

(c) Wren Síofra Lloyd

My Daily Workout   Date.   /   /

I notice a fear that

* ....[Breathe it out]
* ....[Breathe it out]
* ....[Breathe it out]
* ....[Breathe it out]
* ....[Breathe it out]

I notice these judgments about others

* ....[Breathe it out]
* ....[Breathe it out]

Two things I'm accepting & affirming about myself

* ....
* ....

One Way in which I've been playing the martyr

* ....[Breathe it out]

In reality I am: ....

Today I feel obliged to

* ....[Breathe it out]

My work-around: ....
* ....[Breathe it out]

My work-around: ....

Today I Need [for me]

* ....

My work-around: ....
* ....

My work-around: ....
* ....

My work-around: ....

[Use the extension pages at the back of this workbook if you need to do more]

(c) Wren Síofra Lloyd

My Daily Workout   Date.   /   /

I notice a fear that

* ....[Breathe it out]
* ....[Breathe it out]
* ....[Breathe it out]
* ....[Breathe it out]
* ....[Breathe it out]

I notice these judgments about others

* ....[Breathe it out]
* ....[Breathe it out]

Two things I'm accepting & affirming about myself

* ....
* ....

One Way in which I've been playing the martyr

* ....[Breathe it out]

In reality I am: ....

Today I feel obliged to

* ....[Breathe it out]

My work-around: ....
* ....[Breathe it out]

My work-around: ....

Today I Need [for me]

* ....

My work-around: ....
* ....

My work-around: ....
* ....

My work-around: ....

[Use the extension pages at the back of this workbook if you need to do more]

(c) Wren Síofra Lloyd

My Daily Workout   Date.   /   /

I notice a fear that
* ....[Breathe it out]
* ....[Breathe it out]
* ....[Breathe it out]
* ....[Breathe it out]
* ....[Breathe it out]

I notice these judgments about others
* ....[Breathe it out]
* ....[Breathe it out]

Two things I'm accepting & affirming about myself
* ....
* ....

One Way in which I've been playing the martyr
* ....[Breathe it out]

In reality I am: ....

Today I feel obliged to
* ....[Breathe it out]

My work-around: ....
* ....[Breathe it out]

My work-around: ....

Today I Need [for me]
* ....

My work-around: ....
* ....

My work-around: ....
* ....

My work-around: ....

[Use the extension pages at the back of this workbook if you need to do more]

(c) Wren Síofra Lloyd

My Daily Workout   Date.   /   /

I notice a fear that

* ....[Breathe it out]
* ....[Breathe it out]
* ....[Breathe it out]
* ....[Breathe it out]
* ....[Breathe it out]

I notice these judgments about others

* ....[Breathe it out]
* ....[Breathe it out]

Two things I'm accepting & affirming about myself

* ....
* ....
....

One Way in which I've been playing the martyr

* ....[Breathe it out]
In reality I am: ....

Today I feel obliged to

* ....[Breathe it out]
My work-around: ....
* ....[Breathe it out]
My work-around: ....

Today I Need [for me]

* ....
My work-around: ....
* ....
My work-around: ....
* ....
My work-around: ....

[Use the extension pages at the back of this workbook if you need to do more]

(c) Wren Síofra Lloyd

My Week

To Discover Value We Must Evaluate

"One of the best guides
to how to be self-loving is to
give ourselves the love
we are often dreaming about
receiving from others."

~ Bell Hooks

This week's anxiety score: out of 10 =

How does it compare to last week?

This week's 'shame' score: out of 10 =

How does to compare to last week?

What challenges did you overcome?

Did you begin to see any surprising changes?

My Daily Workout   Date.   /   /

I notice a fear that

* ....[Breathe it out]
* ....[Breathe it out]
* ....[Breathe it out]
* ....[Breathe it out]
* ....[Breathe it out]

I notice these judgments about others

* ....[Breathe it out]
* ....[Breathe it out]

Two things I'm accepting & affirming about myself

* ....
* ....

One Way in which I've been playing the martyr

* ....[Breathe it out]

In reality I am: ....

Today I feel obliged to

* ....[Breathe it out]

My work-around: ....
* ....[Breathe it out]

My work-around: ....

Today I Need [for me]

* ....

My work-around: ....
* ....

My work-around: ....
* ....

My work-around: ....

[Use the extension pages at the back of this workbook if you need to do more]

(c) Wren Síofra Lloyd

My Daily Workout   Date.   /   /

I notice a fear that
* ....[Breathe it out]
* ....[Breathe it out]
* ....[Breathe it out]
* ....[Breathe it out]
* ....[Breathe it out]

I notice these judgments about others
* ....[Breathe it out]
* ....[Breathe it out]

Two things I'm accepting & affirming about myself
* ....
* ....

One Way in which I've been playing the martyr
* ....[Breathe it out]

In reality I am: ....

Today I feel obliged to
* ....[Breathe it out]

My work-around: ....
* ....[Breathe it out]

My work-around: ....

Today I Need [for me]
* ....

My work-around: ....
* ....

My work-around: ....
* ....

My work-around: ....

[Use the extension pages at the back of this workbook if you need to do more]

(c) Wren Síofra Lloyd

My Daily Workout

Date.   /   /

I notice a fear that

* ....[Breathe it out]
* ....[Breathe it out]
* ....[Breathe it out]
* ....[Breathe it out]
* ....[Breathe it out]

I notice these judgments about others

* ....[Breathe it out]
* ....[Breathe it out]

Two things I'm accepting & affirming about myself

* ....
* ....

One Way in which I've been playing the martyr

* ....[Breathe it out]

In reality I am: ....

Today I feel obliged to

* ....[Breathe it out]

My work-around: ....
* ....[Breathe it out]

My work-around: ....

Today I Need [for me]

* ....

My work-around: ....
* ....

My work-around: ....
* ....

My work-around: ....

[Use the extension pages at the back of this workbook if you need to do more]

(c) Wren Síofra Lloyd

My Daily Workout   Date.   /   /

I notice a fear that
* ....[Breathe it out]
* ....[Breathe it out]
* ....[Breathe it out]
* ....[Breathe it out]
* ....[Breathe it out]

I notice these judgments about others
* ....[Breathe it out]
* ....[Breathe it out]

Two things I'm accepting & affirming about myself
* ....
* ....

One Way in which I've been playing the martyr
* ....[Breathe it out]

In reality I am: ....

Today I feel obliged to
* ....[Breathe it out]

My work-around: ....
* ....[Breathe it out]

My work-around: ....

Today I Need [for me]
* ....

My work-around: ....
* ....

My work-around: ....
* ....

My work-around: ....

[Use the extension pages at the back of this workbook if you need to do more]

(c) Wren Síofra Lloyd

My Daily Workout   Date.   /   /

I notice a fear that

* ....[Breathe it out]
* ....[Breathe it out]
* ....[Breathe it out]
* ....[Breathe it out]
* ....[Breathe it out]

I notice these judgments about others

* ....[Breathe it out]
* ....[Breathe it out]

Two things I'm accepting & affirming about myself

* ....
* ....

One Way in which I've been playing the martyr

* ....[Breathe it out]

In reality I am: ....

Today I feel obliged to

* ....[Breathe it out]

My work-around: ....
* ....[Breathe it out]

My work-around: ....

Today I Need [for me]

* ....

My work-around: ....
* ....

My work-around: ....
* ....

My work-around: ....

[Use the extension pages at the back of this workbook if you need to do more]

(c) Wren Síofra Lloyd

My Daily Workout   Date.   /   /

I notice a fear that

* ....[Breathe it out]

* ....[Breathe it out]

* ....[Breathe it out]

* ....[Breathe it out]

* ....[Breathe it out]

I notice these judgments about others

* ....[Breathe it out]

* ....[Breathe it out]

Two things I'm accepting & affirming about myself

* ....

* ....

One Way in which I've been playing the martyr

* ....[Breathe it out]

In reality I am: ....

Today I feel obliged to

* ....[Breathe it out]

My work-around: ....

* ....[Breathe it out]

My work-around: ....

Today I Need [for me]

* ....

My work-around: ....

* ....

My work-around: ....

* ....

My work-around: ....

[Use the extension pages at the back of this workbook if you need to do more]

(c) Wren Síofra Lloyd

My Daily Workout

Date.   /   /

I notice a fear that

* ....[Breathe it out]
* ....[Breathe it out]
* ....[Breathe it out]
* ....[Breathe it out]
* ....[Breathe it out]

I notice these judgments about others

* ....[Breathe it out]
* ....[Breathe it out]

Two things I'm accepting & affirming about myself

* ....
* ....

One Way in which I've been playing the martyr

* ....[Breathe it out]

In reality I am: ....

Today I feel obliged to

* ....[Breathe it out]

My work-around: ....

* ....[Breathe it out]

My work-around: ....

Today I Need [for me]

* ....

My work-around: ....

* ....

My work-around: ....

* ....

My work-around: ....

[Use the extension pages at the back of this workbook if you need to do more]

(c) Wren Síofra Lloyd

My Week

To Discover Value We Must Evaluate

"How you love yourself
is how you teach others to
love you."

~ Rupi Kaur

This week's anxiety score: out of 10 =

How does it compare to last week?

This week's 'shame' score: out of 10 =

How does to compare to last week?

What challenges did you overcome?

Did you begin to see any surprising changes?

(c) Wren Síofra Lloyd

My Daily Workout   Date.   /   /

I notice a fear that

* ....[Breathe it out]
* ....[Breathe it out]
* ....[Breathe it out]
* ....[Breathe it out]
* ....[Breathe it out]

I notice these judgments about others

* ....[Breathe it out]
* ....[Breathe it out]

Two things I'm accepting & affirming about myself

* ....
* ....

One Way in which I've been playing the martyr

* ....[Breathe it out]

In reality I am: ....

Today I feel obliged to

* ....[Breathe it out]

My work-around: ....
* ....[Breathe it out]

My work-around: ....

Today I Need [for me]

* ....

My work-around: ....
* ....

My work-around: ....
* ....

My work-around: ....

[Use the extension pages at the back of this workbook if you need to do more]

(c) Wren Síofra Lloyd

My Daily Workout   Date.   /   /

I notice a fear that

* ....[Breathe it out]
* ....[Breathe it out]
* ....[Breathe it out]
* ....[Breathe it out]
* ....[Breathe it out]

I notice these judgments about others

* ....[Breathe it out]
* ....[Breathe it out]

Two things I'm accepting & affirming about myself

* ....
* ....

One Way in which I've been playing the martyr

* ....[Breathe it out]

In reality I am: ....

Today I feel obliged to

* ....[Breathe it out]

My work-around: ....
* ....[Breathe it out]

My work-around: ....

Today I Need [for me]

* ....

My work-around: ....
* ....

My work-around: ....
* ....

My work-around: ....

[Use the extension pages at the back of this workbook if you need to do more]

(c) Wren Síofra Lloyd

My Daily Workout

Date. / /

I notice a fear that

* ....[Breathe it out]
* ....[Breathe it out]
* ....[Breathe it out]
* ....[Breathe it out]
* ....[Breathe it out]

I notice these judgments about others

* ....[Breathe it out]
* ....[Breathe it out]

Two things I'm accepting & affirming about myself

* ....
* ....

One Way in which I've been playing the martyr

* ....[Breathe it out]

In reality I am: ....

Today I feel obliged to

* ....[Breathe it out]

My work-around: ....

* ....[Breathe it out]

My work-around: ....

Today I Need [for me]

* ....

My work-around: ....

* ....

My work-around: ....

* ....

My work-around: ....

[Use the extension pages at the back of this workbook if you need to do more]

(c) Wren Síofra Lloyd

My Daily Workout   Date.   /   /

I notice a fear that
* ....[Breathe it out]
* ....[Breathe it out]
* ....[Breathe it out]
* ....[Breathe it out]
* ....[Breathe it out]

I notice these judgments about others
* ....[Breathe it out]
* ....[Breathe it out]

Two things I'm accepting & affirming about myself
* ....
* ....

One Way in which I've been playing the martyr
* ....[Breathe it out]

In reality I am: ....

Today I feel obliged to
* ....[Breathe it out]

My work-around: ....
* ....[Breathe it out]

My work-around: ....

Today I Need [for me]
* ....

My work-around: ....
* ....

My work-around: ....
* ....

My work-around: ....

[Use the extension pages at the back of this workbook if you need to do more]

(c) Wren Síofra Lloyd

My Daily Workout   Date.   /   /

I notice a fear that

* ....[Breathe it out]
* ....[Breathe it out]
* ....[Breathe it out]
....
* ....[Breathe it out]
....
* ....[Breathe it out]
....

I notice these judgments about others

* ....[Breathe it out]
....
* ....[Breathe it out]
....

Two things I'm accepting & affirming about myself

* ....
* ....
....

One Way in which I've been playing the martyr

* ....[Breathe it out]
In reality I am: ....

Today I feel obliged to

* ....[Breathe it out]
My work-around: ....
* ....[Breathe it out]
My work-around: ....

Today I Need [for me]

* ....
My work-around: ....
* ....
My work-around: ....
* ....
My work-around: ....

[Use the extension pages at the back of this workbook if you need to do more]

(c) Wren Síofra Lloyd

My Daily Workout   Date.   /   /

I notice a fear that
* ....[Breathe it out]
* ....[Breathe it out]
* ....[Breathe it out]
* ....[Breathe it out]
* ....[Breathe it out]

I notice these judgments about others
* ....[Breathe it out]
* ....[Breathe it out]

Two things I'm accepting & affirming about myself
* ....
* ....

One Way in which I've been playing the martyr
* ....[Breathe it out]

In reality I am: ....

Today I feel obliged to
* ....[Breathe it out]

My work-around: ....
* ....[Breathe it out]

My work-around: ....

Today I Need [for me]
* ....

My work-around: ....
* ....

My work-around: ....
* ....

My work-around: ....

[Use the extension pages at the back of this workbook if you need to do more]

(c) Wren Síofra Lloyd

My Daily Workout Date. / /

I notice a fear that

* ....[Breathe it out]
* ....[Breathe it out]
* ....[Breathe it out]
* ....[Breathe it out]
* ....[Breathe it out]

I notice these judgments about others

* ....[Breathe it out]
* ....[Breathe it out]

Two things I'm accepting & affirming about myself

* ....
* ....

One Way in which I've been playing the martyr

* ....[Breathe it out]

In reality I am: ....

Today I feel obliged to

* ....[Breathe it out]

My work-around: ....

* ....[Breathe it out]

My work-around: ....

Today I Need [for me]

* ....

My work-around: ....

* ....

My work-around: ....

* ....

My work-around: ....

[Use the extension pages at the back of this workbook if you need to do more]

(c) Wren Síofra Lloyd

My Week

To Discover Value We Must Evaluate

"As I began to love myself,
I found that anguish and
emotional suffering
were only warning signs
that I was living
against my own truth."
~ Charlie Chaplin

This week's anxiety score: out of 10 =

How does it compare to last week?

This week's 'shame' score: out of 10 =

How does to compare to last week?

What challenges did you overcome?

Did you begin to see any surprising changes?

(c) Wren Síofra Lloyd

My Daily Workout   Date.   /   /

I notice a fear that
* ....[Breathe it out]
* ....[Breathe it out]
* ....[Breathe it out]
* ....[Breathe it out]
* ....[Breathe it out]

I notice these judgments about others
* ....[Breathe it out]
* ....[Breathe it out]

Two things I'm accepting & affirming about myself
* ....
* ....

One Way in which I've been playing the martyr
* ....[Breathe it out]
In reality I am: ....

Today I feel obliged to
* ....[Breathe it out]
My work-around: ....
* ....[Breathe it out]
My work-around: ....

Today I Need [for me]
* ....
My work-around: ....
* ....
My work-around: ....
* ....
My work-around: ....

[Use the extension pages at the back of this workbook if you need to do more]

(c) Wren Síofra Lloyd

My Daily Workout   Date.   /   /

I notice a fear that
* ....[Breathe it out]
* ....[Breathe it out]
* ....[Breathe it out]
* ....[Breathe it out]
* ....[Breathe it out]

I notice these judgments about others
* ....[Breathe it out]
* ....[Breathe it out]

Two things I'm accepting & affirming about myself
* ....
* ....

One Way in which I've been playing the martyr
* ....[Breathe it out]

In reality I am: ....

Today I feel obliged to
* ....[Breathe it out]

My work-around: ....
* ....[Breathe it out]

My work-around: ....

Today I Need [for me]
* ....

My work-around: ....
* ....

My work-around: ....
* ....

My work-around: ....

[Use the extension pages at the back of this workbook if you need to do more]

(c) Wren Síofra Lloyd

My Daily Workout Date. / /

I notice a fear that

* ....[Breathe it out]
* ....[Breathe it out]
* ....[Breathe it out]
* ....[Breathe it out]
* ....[Breathe it out]

I notice these judgments about others

* ....[Breathe it out]
* ....[Breathe it out]

Two things I'm accepting & affirming about myself

* ....
* ....

One Way in which I've been playing the martyr

* ....[Breathe it out]

In reality I am: ....

Today I feel obliged to

* ....[Breathe it out]

My work-around: ....

* ....[Breathe it out]

My work-around: ....

Today I Need [for me]

* ....

My work-around: ....

* ....

My work-around: ....

* ....

My work-around: ....

[Use the extension pages at the back of this workbook if you need to do more]

(c) Wren Síofra Lloyd

My Daily Workout   Date.   /   /

I notice a fear that

* ....[Breathe it out]
* ....[Breathe it out]
* ....[Breathe it out]
* ....[Breathe it out]
* ....[Breathe it out]

I notice these judgments about others

* ....[Breathe it out]
* ....[Breathe it out]

Two things I'm accepting & affirming about myself

* ....
* ....

One Way in which I've been playing the martyr

* ....[Breathe it out]

In reality I am: ....

Today I feel obliged to

* ....[Breathe it out]

My work-around: ....
* ....[Breathe it out]

My work-around: ....

Today I Need [for me]

* ....

My work-around: ....
* ....

My work-around: ....
* ....

My work-around: ....

[Use the extension pages at the back of this workbook if you need to do more]

(c) Wren Síofra Lloyd

My Daily Workout   Date.   /   /

I notice a fear that

* ....[Breathe it out]
* ....[Breathe it out]
* ....[Breathe it out]
* ....[Breathe it out]
* ....[Breathe it out]

I notice these judgments about others

* ....[Breathe it out]
* ....[Breathe it out]

Two things I'm accepting & affirming about myself

* ....
* ....

One Way in which I've been playing the martyr

* ....[Breathe it out]

In reality I am: ....

Today I feel obliged to

* ....[Breathe it out]

My work-around: ....
* ....[Breathe it out]

My work-around: ....

Today I Need [for me]

* ....

My work-around: ....
* ....

My work-around: ....
* ....

My work-around: ....

[Use the extension pages at the back of this workbook if you need to do more]

(c) Wren Síofra Lloyd

My Daily Workout   Date.   /   /

I notice a fear that
* ....[Breathe it out]
* ....[Breathe it out]
* ....[Breathe it out]
* ....[Breathe it out]
* ....[Breathe it out]

I notice these judgments about others
* ....[Breathe it out]
* ....[Breathe it out]

Two things I'm accepting & affirming about myself
* ....
* ....

One Way in which I've been playing the martyr
* ....[Breathe it out]

In reality I am: ....

Today I feel obliged to
* ....[Breathe it out]

My work-around: ....

* ....[Breathe it out]

My work-around: ....

Today I Need [for me]
* ....

My work-around: ....

* ....

My work-around: ....

* ....

My work-around: ....

[Use the extension pages at the back of this workbook if you need to do more]

(c) Wren Síofra Lloyd

My Daily Workout

Date. / /

I notice a fear that

* ....[Breathe it out]

* ....[Breathe it out]

* ....[Breathe it out]

* ....[Breathe it out]

* ....[Breathe it out]

I notice these judgments about others

* ....[Breathe it out]

* ....[Breathe it out]

Two things I'm accepting & affirming about myself

* ....

* ....

One Way in which I've been playing the martyr

* ....[Breathe it out]

In reality I am: ....

Today I feel obliged to

* ....[Breathe it out]

My work-around: ....

* ....[Breathe it out]

My work-around: ....

Today I Need [for me]

* ....

My work-around: ....

* ....

My work-around: ....

* ....

My work-around: ....

[Use the extension pages at the back of this workbook if you need to do more]

(c) Wren Síofra Lloyd

My Week

To Discover Value We Must Evaluate

"The absence of self-love can
never be replaced with
the presence of people's
love for you."
~ Edmond Mbiaka

This week's anxiety score: out of 10 =

How does it compare to last week?

This week's 'shame' score: out of 10 =

How does to compare to last week?

What challenges did you overcome?

Did you begin to see any surprising changes?

(c) Wren Síofra Lloyd

My Week

To Discover Value We Must Evaluate

"The absence of self-love can
never be replaced with
the presence of people's
love for you."
~ Edmond Mbiaka

This week's anxiety score: out of 10 =

How does it compare to last week?

This week's 'shame' score: out of 10 =

How does to compare to last week?

What challenges did you overcome?

Did you begin to see any surprising changes?

(c) Wren Síofra Lloyd

My Daily Workout   Date.   /   /

I notice a fear that

* ....[Breathe it out]
* ....[Breathe it out]
* ....[Breathe it out]
* ....[Breathe it out]
* ....[Breathe it out]

I notice these judgments about others

* ....[Breathe it out]
* ....[Breathe it out]

Two things I'm accepting & affirming about myself

* ....
* ....

One Way in which I've been playing the martyr

* ....[Breathe it out]

In reality I am: ....

Today I feel obliged to

* ....[Breathe it out]

My work-around: ....
* ....[Breathe it out]

My work-around: ....

Today I Need [for me]

* ....

My work-around: ....
* ....

My work-around: ....
* ....

My work-around: ....

[Use the extension pages at the back of this workbook if you need to do more]

(c) Wren Síofra Lloyd

My Daily Workout   Date.   /   /

I notice a fear that

* ....[Breathe it out]
* ....[Breathe it out]
* ....[Breathe it out]
* ....[Breathe it out]
* ....[Breathe it out]

I notice these judgments about others

* ....[Breathe it out]
* ....[Breathe it out]

Two things I'm accepting & affirming about myself

* ....

* ....
....

One Way in which I've been playing the martyr

* ....[Breathe it out]
In reality I am: ....

Today I feel obliged to

* ....[Breathe it out]
My work-around: ....
* ....[Breathe it out]
My work-around: ....

Today I Need [for me]

* ....
My work-around: ....
* ....
My work-around: ....
* ....
My work-around: ....

[Use the extension pages at the back of this workbook if you need to do more]

(c) Wren Síofra Lloyd

My Daily Workout   Date.   /   /

I notice a fear that

* ....[Breathe it out]
* ....[Breathe it out]
* ....[Breathe it out]
* ....[Breathe it out]
* ....[Breathe it out]

I notice these judgments about others

* ....[Breathe it out]
* ....[Breathe it out]

Two things I'm accepting & affirming about myself

* ....
* ....

One Way in which I've been playing the martyr

* ....[Breathe it out]

In reality I am: ....

Today I feel obliged to

* ....[Breathe it out]

My work-around: ....
* ....[Breathe it out]

My work-around: ....

Today I Need [for me]

* ....

My work-around: ....
* ....

My work-around: ....
* ....

My work-around: ....

[Use the extension pages at the back of this workbook if you need to do more]

(c) Wren Síofra Lloyd

My Daily Workout   Date.   /   /

I notice a fear that

* ....[Breathe it out]
* ....[Breathe it out]
* ....[Breathe it out]
* ....[Breathe it out]
* ....[Breathe it out]

I notice these judgments about others

* ....[Breathe it out]
* ....[Breathe it out]

Two things I'm accepting & affirming about myself

* ....
* ....

One Way in which I've been playing the martyr

* ....[Breathe it out]

In reality I am: ....

Today I feel obliged to

* ....[Breathe it out]

My work-around: ....
* ....[Breathe it out]

My work-around: ....

Today I Need [for me]

* ....

My work-around: ....
* ....

My work-around: ....
* ....

My work-around: ....

[Use the extension pages at the back of this workbook if you need to do more]

(c) Wren Síofra Lloyd

My Daily Workout   Date.   /   /

I notice a fear that
* ....[Breathe it out]
* ....[Breathe it out]
* ....[Breathe it out]
* ....[Breathe it out]
* ....[Breathe it out]

I notice these judgments about others
* ....[Breathe it out]
* ....[Breathe it out]

Two things I'm accepting & affirming about myself
* ....
* ....

One Way in which I've been playing the martyr
* ....[Breathe it out]
In reality I am: ....

Today I feel obliged to
* ....[Breathe it out]
My work-around: ....
* ....[Breathe it out]
My work-around: ....

Today I Need [for me]
* ....
My work-around: ....
* ....
My work-around: ....
* ....
My work-around: ....

[Use the extension pages at the back of this workbook if you need to do more]

(c) Wren Síofra Lloyd

My Daily Workout   Date.   /   /

I notice a fear that

* ....[Breathe it out]

* ....[Breathe it out]

* ....[Breathe it out]

* ....[Breathe it out]

* ....[Breathe it out]

I notice these judgments about others

* ....[Breathe it out]

* ....[Breathe it out]

Two things I'm accepting & affirming about myself

* ....

* ....

One Way in which I've been playing the martyr

* ....[Breathe it out]

In reality I am: ....

Today I feel obliged to

* ....[Breathe it out]

My work-around: ....

* ....[Breathe it out]

My work-around: ....

Today I Need [for me]

* ....

My work-around: ....

* ....

My work-around: ....

* ....

My work-around: ....

[Use the extension pages at the back of this workbook if you need to do more]

(c) Wren Síofra Lloyd

My Daily Workout   Date.   /   /

I notice a fear that

* ....[Breathe it out]
* ....[Breathe it out]
* ....[Breathe it out]
* ....[Breathe it out]
* ....[Breathe it out]

I notice these judgments about others

* ....[Breathe it out]
* ....[Breathe it out]

Two things I'm accepting & affirming about myself

* ....
  ....
* ....
  ....

One Way in which I've been playing the martyr

* ....[Breathe it out]

In reality I am: ....

Today I feel obliged to

* ....[Breathe it out]

My work-around: ....
* ....[Breathe it out]

My work-around: ....

Today I Need [for me]

* ....

My work-around: ....
* ....

My work-around: ....
* ....

My work-around: ....

[Use the extension pages at the back of this workbook if you need to do more]

(c) Wren Síofra Lloyd

My Week

To Discover Value We Must Evaluate

"All people deserve
your kindness, but none
more so than you."

~ Justin Kan

This week's anxiety score: out of 10 =

How does it compare to last week?

This week's 'shame' score: out of 10 =

How does to compare to last week?

What challenges did you overcome?

Did you begin to see any surprising changes?

(c) Wren Síofra Lloyd

My Daily Workout   Date. / /

I notice a fear that
* ....[Breathe it out]
* ....[Breathe it out]
* ....[Breathe it out]
* ....[Breathe it out]
* ....[Breathe it out]

I notice these judgments about others
* ....[Breathe it out]
* ....[Breathe it out]

Two things I'm accepting & affirming about myself
* ....
* ....

One Way in which I've been playing the martyr
* ....[Breathe it out]
In reality I am: ....

Today I feel obliged to
* ....[Breathe it out]
My work-around: ....
* ....[Breathe it out]
My work-around: ....

Today I Need [for me]
* ....
My work-around: ....
* ....
My work-around: ....
* ....
My work-around: ....

[Use the extension pages at the back of this workbook if you need to do more]

(c) Wren Síofra Lloyd

My Daily Workout   Date.   /   /

I notice a fear that

* ....[Breathe it out]
* ....[Breathe it out]
* ....[Breathe it out]
* ....[Breathe it out]
* ....[Breathe it out]

I notice these judgments about others

* ....[Breathe it out]
* ....[Breathe it out]

Two things I'm accepting & affirming about myself

* ....
* ....

One Way in which I've been playing the martyr

* ....[Breathe it out]

In reality I am: ....

Today I feel obliged to

* ....[Breathe it out]

My work-around: ....
* ....[Breathe it out]

My work-around: ....

Today I Need [for me]

* ....

My work-around: ....
* ....

My work-around: ....
* ....

My work-around: ....

[Use the extension pages at the back of this workbook if you need to do more]

(c) Wren Síofra Lloyd

My Daily Workout   Date.   /   /

I notice a fear that

* ....[Breathe it out]
* ....[Breathe it out]
* ....[Breathe it out]
* ....[Breathe it out]
* ....[Breathe it out]

I notice these judgments about others

* ....[Breathe it out]
* ....[Breathe it out]

Two things I'm accepting & affirming about myself

* ....
* ....

One Way in which I've been playing the martyr

* ....[Breathe it out]

In reality I am: ....

Today I feel obliged to

* ....[Breathe it out]

My work-around: ....
* ....[Breathe it out]

My work-around: ....

Today I Need [for me]

* ....

My work-around: ....
* ....

My work-around: ....
* ....

My work-around: ....

[Use the extension pages at the back of this workbook if you need to do more]

(c) Wren Síofra Lloyd

My Daily Workout

Date. / /

I notice a fear that

* ....[Breathe it out]
* ....[Breathe it out]
* ....[Breathe it out]
* ....[Breathe it out]
* ....[Breathe it out]

I notice these judgments about others

* ....[Breathe it out]
* ....[Breathe it out]

Two things I'm accepting & affirming about myself

* ....
* ....

One Way in which I've been playing the martyr

* ....[Breathe it out]

In reality I am: ....

Today I feel obliged to

* ....[Breathe it out]

My work-around: ....
* ....[Breathe it out]

My work-around: ....

Today I Need [for me]

* ....

My work-around: ....
* ....

My work-around: ....
* ....

My work-around: ....

[Use the extension pages at the back of this workbook if you need to do more]

(c) Wren Síofra Lloyd

My Daily Workout   Date.   /   /

I notice a fear that
* ....[Breathe it out]
* ....[Breathe it out]
* ....[Breathe it out]
* ....[Breathe it out]
* ....[Breathe it out]

I notice these judgments about others
* ....[Breathe it out]
* ....[Breathe it out]

Two things I'm accepting & affirming about myself
* ....
* ....

One Way in which I've been playing the martyr
* ....[Breathe it out]
In reality I am: ....

Today I feel obliged to
* ....[Breathe it out]
My work-around: ....
* ....[Breathe it out]
My work-around: ....

Today I Need [for me]
* ....
My work-around: ....
* ....
My work-around: ....
* ....
My work-around: ....

[Use the extension pages at the back of this workbook if you need to do more]

(c) Wren Síofra Lloyd

My Daily Workout

Date. / /

I notice a fear that

* ....[Breathe it out]
* ....[Breathe it out]
* ....[Breathe it out]
* ....[Breathe it out]
* ....[Breathe it out]

I notice these judgments about others

* ....[Breathe it out]
* ....[Breathe it out]

Two things I'm accepting & affirming about myself

* ....
* ....

One Way in which I've been playing the martyr

* ....[Breathe it out]

In reality I am: ....

Today I feel obliged to

* ....[Breathe it out]

My work-around: ....

* ....[Breathe it out]

My work-around: ....

Today I Need [for me]

* ....

My work-around: ....

* ....

My work-around: ....

* ....

My work-around: ....

[Use the extension pages at the back of this workbook if you need to do more]

(c) Wren Síofra Lloyd

My Daily Workout   Date.   /   /

I notice a fear that

* ....[Breathe it out]
* ....[Breathe it out]
* ....[Breathe it out]
* ....[Breathe it out]
* ....[Breathe it out]

I notice these judgments about others

* ....[Breathe it out]
* ....[Breathe it out]

Two things I'm accepting & affirming about myself

* ....
* ....

One Way in which I've been playing the martyr

* ....[Breathe it out]

In reality I am: ....

Today I feel obliged to

* ....[Breathe it out]

My work-around: ....
* ....[Breathe it out]

My work-around: ....

Today I Need [for me]

* ....

My work-around: ....
* ....

My work-around: ....
* ....

My work-around: ....

[Use the extension pages at the back of this workbook if you need to do more]

(c) Wren Síofra Lloyd

My Week

To Discover Value We Must Evaluate

"Self-love is the source of all
our other loves."

~ Pierre Corneille

This week's anxiety score: out of 10 =

How does it compare to last week?

This week's 'shame' score: out of 10 =

How does to compare to last week?

What challenges did you overcome?

Did you begin to see any surprising changes?

(c) Wren Síofra Lloyd

My Daily Workout   Date.   /   /

I notice a fear that
* ....[Breathe it out]
* ....[Breathe it out]
* ....[Breathe it out]
* ....[Breathe it out]
* ....[Breathe it out]

I notice these judgments about others
* ....[Breathe it out]
* ....[Breathe it out]

Two things I'm accepting & affirming about myself
* ....
* ....

One Way in which I've been playing the martyr
* ....[Breathe it out]
In reality I am: ....

Today I feel obliged to
* ....[Breathe it out]
My work-around: ....
* ....[Breathe it out]
My work-around: ....

Today I Need [for me]
* ....
My work-around: ....
* ....
My work-around: ....
* ....
My work-around: ....

[Use the extension pages at the back of this workbook if you need to do more]

(c) Wren Síofra Lloyd

My Daily Workout   Date.   /   /

I notice a fear that

* ....[Breathe it out]
* ....[Breathe it out]
* ....[Breathe it out]
* ....[Breathe it out]
* ....[Breathe it out]

I notice these judgments about others

* ....[Breathe it out]
* ....[Breathe it out]

Two things I'm accepting & affirming about myself

* ....

* ....

One Way in which I've been playing the martyr

* ....[Breathe it out]

In reality I am: ....

Today I feel obliged to

* ....[Breathe it out]

My work-around: ....
* ....[Breathe it out]

My work-around: ....

Today I Need [for me]

* ....

My work-around: ....
* ....

My work-around: ....
* ....

My work-around: ....

[Use the extension pages at the back of this workbook if you need to do more]

(c) Wren Síofra Lloyd

My Daily Workout   Date.   /   /

I notice a fear that
* ....[Breathe it out]
* ....[Breathe it out]
* ....[Breathe it out]
* ....[Breathe it out]
* ....[Breathe it out]

I notice these judgments about others
* ....[Breathe it out]
* ....[Breathe it out]

Two things I'm accepting & affirming about myself
* ....
* ....

One Way in which I've been playing the martyr
* ....[Breathe it out]
In reality I am: ....

Today I feel obliged to
* ....[Breathe it out]
My work-around: ....
* ....[Breathe it out]
My work-around: ....

Today I Need [for me]
* ....
My work-around: ....
* ....
My work-around: ....
* ....
My work-around: ....

[Use the extension pages at the back of this workbook if you need to do more]

(c) Wren Síofra Lloyd

My Daily Workout   Date.   /   /

I notice a fear that
* ....[Breathe it out]
* ....[Breathe it out]
* ....[Breathe it out]
* ....[Breathe it out]
* ....[Breathe it out]

I notice these judgments about others
* ....[Breathe it out]
* ....[Breathe it out]

Two things I'm accepting & affirming about myself
* ....
* ....

One Way in which I've been playing the martyr
* ....[Breathe it out]
In reality I am: ....

Today I feel obliged to
* ....[Breathe it out]
My work-around: ....
* ....[Breathe it out]
My work-around: ....

Today I Need [for me]
* ....
My work-around: ....
* ....
My work-around: ....
* ....
My work-around: ....

[Use the extension pages at the back of this workbook if you need to do more]

(c) Wren Síofra Lloyd

My Daily Workout   Date.   /   /

I notice a fear that

* ....[Breathe it out]
* ....[Breathe it out]
* ....[Breathe it out]
* ....[Breathe it out]
* ....[Breathe it out]

I notice these judgments about others

* ....[Breathe it out]
* ....[Breathe it out]

Two things I'm accepting & affirming about myself

* ....
* ....

One Way in which I've been playing the martyr

* ....[Breathe it out]
In reality I am: ....

Today I feel obliged to

* ....[Breathe it out]
My work-around: ....
* ....[Breathe it out]
My work-around: ....

Today I Need [for me]

* ....
My work-around: ....
* ....
My work-around: ....
* ....
My work-around: ....

[Use the extension pages at the back of this workbook if you need to do more]

(c) Wren Síofra Lloyd

My Daily Workout   Date.   /   /

I notice a fear that
* ....[Breathe it out]
* ....[Breathe it out]
* ....[Breathe it out]
* ....[Breathe it out]
* ....[Breathe it out]

I notice these judgments about others
* ....[Breathe it out]
* ....[Breathe it out]

Two things I'm accepting & affirming about myself
* ....
* ....

One Way in which I've been playing the martyr
* ....[Breathe it out]

In reality I am: ....

Today I feel obliged to
* ....[Breathe it out]

My work-around: ....
* ....[Breathe it out]

My work-around: ....

Today I Need [for me]
* ....

My work-around: ....
* ....

My work-around: ....
* ....

My work-around: ....

[Use the extension pages at the back of this workbook if you need to do more]

(c) Wren Síofra Lloyd

My Daily Workout   Date.   /   /

I notice a fear that
* ....[Breathe it out]
* ....[Breathe it out]
* ....[Breathe it out]
* ....[Breathe it out]
* ....[Breathe it out]

I notice these judgments about others
* ....[Breathe it out]
* ....[Breathe it out]

Two things I'm accepting & affirming about myself
* ....
* ....

One Way in which I've been playing the martyr
* ....[Breathe it out]
In reality I am: ....

Today I feel obliged to
* ....[Breathe it out]
My work-around: ....
* ....[Breathe it out]
My work-around: ....

Today I Need [for me]
* ....
My work-around: ....
* ....
My work-around: ....
* ....
My work-around: ....

[Use the extension pages at the back of this workbook if you need to do more]

(c) Wren Síofra Lloyd

My Week

To Discover Value We Must Evaluate

"Most of the shadows
of this life are caused
by standing in
one's own sunshine."
~ Ralph Waldo Emerson

This week's anxiety score: out of 10 =

How does it compare to last week?

This week's 'shame' score: out of 10 =

How does to compare to last week?

What challenges did you overcome?

Did you begin to see any surprising changes?

(c) Wren Síofra Lloyd

My Daily Workout   Date.   /   /

I notice a fear that

* ....[Breathe it out]
* ....[Breathe it out]
* ....[Breathe it out]
* ....[Breathe it out]
* ....[Breathe it out]

I notice these judgments about others

* ....[Breathe it out]
* ....[Breathe it out]

Two things I'm accepting & affirming about myself

* ....
* ....

One Way in which I've been playing the martyr

* ....[Breathe it out]

In reality I am: ....

Today I feel obliged to

* ....[Breathe it out]

My work-around: ....
* ....[Breathe it out]

My work-around: ....

Today I Need [for me]

* ....

My work-around: ....
* ....

My work-around: ....
* ....

My work-around: ....

[Use the extension pages at the back of this workbook if you need to do more]

(c) Wren Síofra Lloyd

My Daily Workout   Date.   /   /

I notice a fear that

* ....[Breathe it out]
* ....[Breathe it out]
* ....[Breathe it out]
* ....[Breathe it out]
* ....[Breathe it out]

I notice these judgments about others

* ....[Breathe it out]
* ....[Breathe it out]

Two things I'm accepting & affirming about myself

* ....
* ....

One Way in which I've been playing the martyr

* ....[Breathe it out]

In reality I am: ....

Today I feel obliged to

* ....[Breathe it out]

My work-around: ....

* ....[Breathe it out]

My work-around: ....

Today I Need [for me]

* ....

My work-around: ....

* ....

My work-around: ....

* ....

My work-around: ....

[Use the extension pages at the back of this workbook if you need to do more]

(c) Wren Síofra Lloyd

My Daily Workout   Date.   /   /

I notice a fear that

* ....[Breathe it out]
* ....[Breathe it out]
* ....[Breathe it out]
* ....[Breathe it out]
* ....[Breathe it out]

I notice these judgments about others

* ....[Breathe it out]
* ....[Breathe it out]

Two things I'm accepting & affirming about myself

* ....
* ....

One Way in which I've been playing the martyr

* ....[Breathe it out]

In reality I am: ....

Today I feel obliged to

* ....[Breathe it out]

My work-around: ....
* ....[Breathe it out]

My work-around: ....

Today I Need [for me]

* ....

My work-around: ....
* ....

My work-around: ....
* ....

My work-around: ....

[Use the extension pages at the back of this workbook if you need to do more]

(c) Wren Síofra Lloyd

My Daily Workout   Date.   /   /

I notice a fear that

* ....[Breathe it out]
* ....[Breathe it out]
* ....[Breathe it out]
* ....[Breathe it out]
* ....[Breathe it out]

I notice these judgments about others

* ....[Breathe it out]
* ....[Breathe it out]

Two things I'm accepting & affirming about myself

* ....
* ....

One Way in which I've been playing the martyr

* ....[Breathe it out]

In reality I am: ....

Today I feel obliged to

* ....[Breathe it out]

My work-around: ....
* ....[Breathe it out]

My work-around: ....

Today I Need [for me]

* ....

My work-around: ....
* ....

My work-around: ....
* ....

My work-around: ....

[Use the extension pages at the back of this workbook if you need to do more]

(c) Wren Síofra Lloyd

My Daily Workout Date. / /

I notice a fear that

* ....[Breathe it out]
* ....[Breathe it out]
* ....[Breathe it out]
* ....[Breathe it out]
* ....[Breathe it out]

I notice these judgments about others

* ....[Breathe it out]
* ....[Breathe it out]

Two things I'm accepting & affirming about myself

* ....
* ....

One Way in which I've been playing the martyr

* ....[Breathe it out]

In reality I am: ....

Today I feel obliged to

* ....[Breathe it out]

My work-around: ....
* ....[Breathe it out]

My work-around: ....

Today I Need [for me]

* ....

My work-around: ....
* ....

My work-around: ....
* ....

My work-around: ....

[Use the extension pages at the back of this workbook if you need to do more]

(c) Wren Síofra Lloyd

My Daily Workout   Date.   /   /

I notice a fear that

* ....[Breathe it out]
* ....[Breathe it out]
* ....[Breathe it out]
* ....[Breathe it out]
* ....[Breathe it out]

I notice these judgments about others

* ....[Breathe it out]
* ....[Breathe it out]

Two things I'm accepting & affirming about myself

* ....
* ....

One Way in which I've been playing the martyr

* ....[Breathe it out]

In reality I am: ....

Today I feel obliged to

* ....[Breathe it out]

My work-around: ....
* ....[Breathe it out]

My work-around: ....

Today I Need [for me]

* ....

My work-around: ....
* ....

My work-around: ....
* ....

My work-around: ....

[Use the extension pages at the back of this workbook if you need to do more]

(c) Wren Síofra Lloyd

My Daily Workout   Date.   /   /

I notice a fear that

* ....[Breathe it out]
* ....[Breathe it out]
* ....[Breathe it out]
* ....[Breathe it out]
* ....[Breathe it out]

I notice these judgments about others

* ....[Breathe it out]
* ....[Breathe it out]

Two things I'm accepting & affirming about myself

* ....
* ....

One Way in which I've been playing the martyr

* ....[Breathe it out]

In reality I am: ....

Today I feel obliged to

* ....[Breathe it out]

My work-around: ....
* ....[Breathe it out]

My work-around: ....

Today I Need [for me]

* ....

My work-around: ....
* ....

My work-around: ....
* ....

My work-around: ....

[Use the extension pages at the back of this workbook if you need to do more]

(c) Wren Síofra Lloyd

My Week

To Discover Value We Must Evaluate

"Love yourself so much that
when someone treats you wrong,
you recognize it."
~ Rena Rose

This week's anxiety score: out of 10 =

How does it compare to last week?

This week's 'shame' score: out of 10 =

How does to compare to last week?

What challenges did you overcome?

Did you begin to see any surprising changes?

(c) Wren Síofra Lloyd

My Daily Workout   Date.   /   /

I notice a fear that
* ....[Breathe it out]
* ....[Breathe it out]
* ....[Breathe it out]
* ....[Breathe it out]
* ....[Breathe it out]

I notice these judgments about others
* ....[Breathe it out]
* ....[Breathe it out]

Two things I'm accepting & affirming about myself
* ....
* ....

One Way in which I've been playing the martyr
* ....[Breathe it out]
In reality I am: ....

Today I feel obliged to
* ....[Breathe it out]
My work-around: ....
* ....[Breathe it out]
My work-around: ....

Today I Need [for me]
* ....
My work-around: ....
* ....
My work-around: ....
* ....
My work-around: ....

[Use the extension pages at the back of this workbook if you need to do more]

(c) Wren Síofra Lloyd

My Daily Workout   Date.   /   /

I notice a fear that
* ....[Breathe it out]
* ....[Breathe it out]
* ....[Breathe it out]
* ....[Breathe it out]
* ....[Breathe it out]

I notice these judgments about others
* ....[Breathe it out]
* ....[Breathe it out]

Two things I'm accepting & affirming about myself
* ....
* ....

One Way in which I've been playing the martyr
* ....[Breathe it out]
In reality I am: ....

Today I feel obliged to
* ....[Breathe it out]
My work-around: ....
* ....[Breathe it out]
My work-around: ....

Today I Need [for me]
* ....
My work-around: ....
* ....
My work-around: ....
* ....
My work-around: ....

[Use the extension pages at the back of this workbook if you need to do more]

(c) Wren Síofra Lloyd

My Daily Workout   Date.   /   /

I notice a fear that
* ....[Breathe it out]
* ....[Breathe it out]
* ....[Breathe it out]
* ....[Breathe it out]
* ....[Breathe it out]

I notice these judgments about others
* ....[Breathe it out]
* ....[Breathe it out]

Two things I'm accepting & affirming about myself
* ....
* ....

One Way in which I've been playing the martyr
* ....[Breathe it out]

In reality I am: ....

Today I feel obliged to
* ....[Breathe it out]

My work-around: ....
* ....[Breathe it out]

My work-around: ....

Today I Need [for me]
* ....

My work-around: ....
* ....

My work-around: ....
* ....

My work-around: ....

[Use the extension pages at the back of this workbook if you need to do more]

(c) Wren Síofra Lloyd

My Daily Workout   Date.   /   /

I notice a fear that
* ....[Breathe it out]
* ....[Breathe it out]
* ....[Breathe it out]
* ....[Breathe it out]
* ....[Breathe it out]

I notice these judgments about others
* ....[Breathe it out]
* ....[Breathe it out]

Two things I'm accepting & affirming about myself
* ....
* ....

One Way in which I've been playing the martyr
* ....[Breathe it out]

In reality I am: ....

Today I feel obliged to
* ....[Breathe it out]

My work-around: ....
* ....[Breathe it out]

My work-around: ....

Today I Need [for me]
* ....

My work-around: ....
* ....

My work-around: ....
* ....

My work-around: ....

[Use the extension pages at the back of this workbook if you need to do more]

(c) Wren Síofra Lloyd

My Daily Workout   Date.   /   /

I notice a fear that

* ....[Breathe it out]
* ....[Breathe it out]
* ....[Breathe it out]
* ....[Breathe it out]
* ....[Breathe it out]

I notice these judgments about others

* ....[Breathe it out]
* ....[Breathe it out]

Two things I'm accepting & affirming about myself

* ....
* ....

One Way in which I've been playing the martyr

* ....[Breathe it out]

In reality I am: ....

Today I feel obliged to

* ....[Breathe it out]

My work-around: ....
* ....[Breathe it out]

My work-around: ....

Today I Need [for me]

* ....

My work-around: ....
* ....

My work-around: ....
* ....

My work-around: ....

[Use the extension pages at the back of this workbook if you need to do more]

(c) Wren Síofra Lloyd

My Daily Workout   Date.   /   /

I notice a fear that
* ....[Breathe it out]
* ....[Breathe it out]
* ....[Breathe it out]
* ....[Breathe it out]
* ....[Breathe it out]

I notice these judgments about others
* ....[Breathe it out]
* ....[Breathe it out]

Two things I'm accepting & affirming about myself
* ....
* ....

One Way in which I've been playing the martyr
* ....[Breathe it out]
In reality I am: ....

Today I feel obliged to
* ....[Breathe it out]
My work-around: ....
* ....[Breathe it out]
My work-around: ....

Today I Need [for me]
* ....
My work-around: ....
* ....
My work-around: ....
* ....
My work-around: ....

[Use the extension pages at the back of this workbook if you need to do more]

(c) Wren Síofra Lloyd

My Daily Workout   Date.   /   /

I notice a fear that

* ....[Breathe it out]
* ....[Breathe it out]
* ....[Breathe it out]
* ....[Breathe it out]
* ....[Breathe it out]

I notice these judgments about others

* ....[Breathe it out]
* ....[Breathe it out]

Two things I'm accepting & affirming about myself

* ....
* ....

One Way in which I've been playing the martyr

* ....[Breathe it out]

In reality I am: ....

Today I feel obliged to

* ....[Breathe it out]

My work-around: ....

* ....[Breathe it out]

My work-around: ....

Today I Need [for me]

* ....

My work-around: ....

* ....

My work-around: ....

* ....

My work-around: ....

[Use the extension pages at the back of this workbook if you need to do more]

(c) Wren Síofra Lloyd

My Week

To Discover Value We Must Evaluate

"You are very powerful,
provided you know how
powerful you are."
~ Yogi Bahaman

This week's anxiety score: out of 10 =

How does it compare to last week?

This week's 'shame' score: out of 10 =

How does to compare to last week?

What challenges did you overcome?

Did you begin to see any surprising changes?

(c) Wren Síofra Lloyd

My Daily Workout   Date.   /   /

I notice a fear that

* ....[Breathe it out]
* ....[Breathe it out]
* ....[Breathe it out]
* ....[Breathe it out]
* ....[Breathe it out]

I notice these judgments about others

* ....[Breathe it out]
* ....[Breathe it out]

Two things I'm accepting & affirming about myself

* ....
* ....

One Way in which I've been playing the martyr

* ....[Breathe it out]

In reality I am: ....

Today I feel obliged to

* ....[Breathe it out]

My work-around: ....
* ....[Breathe it out]

My work-around: ....

Today I Need [for me]

* ....

My work-around: ....
* ....

My work-around: ....
* ....

My work-around: ....

[Use the extension pages at the back of this workbook if you need to do more]

(c) Wren Síofra Lloyd

My Daily Workout   Date.   /   /

I notice a fear that

* ....[Breathe it out]
* ....[Breathe it out]
* ....[Breathe it out]
* ....[Breathe it out]
* ....[Breathe it out]

I notice these judgments about others

* ....[Breathe it out]
* ....[Breathe it out]

Two things I'm accepting & affirming about myself

* ....
* ....

One Way in which I've been playing the martyr

* ....[Breathe it out]
In reality I am: ....

Today I feel obliged to

* ....[Breathe it out]
My work-around: ....
* ....[Breathe it out]
My work-around: ....

Today I Need [for me]

* ....
My work-around: ....
* ....
My work-around: ....
* ....
My work-around: ....

[Use the extension pages at the back of this workbook if you need to do more]

(c) Wren Síofra Lloyd

My Daily Workout

Date. / /

I notice a fear that

* ....[Breathe it out]
* ....[Breathe it out]
* ....[Breathe it out]
* ....[Breathe it out]
* ....[Breathe it out]

I notice these judgments about others

* ....[Breathe it out]
* ....[Breathe it out]

Two things I'm accepting & affirming about myself

* ....
* ....

One Way in which I've been playing the martyr

* ....[Breathe it out]

In reality I am: ....

Today I feel obliged to

* ....[Breathe it out]

My work-around: ....

* ....[Breathe it out]

My work-around: ....

Today I Need [for me]

* ....

My work-around: ....

* ....

My work-around: ....

* ....

My work-around: ....

[Use the extension pages at the back of this workbook if you need to do more]

(c) Wren Síofra Lloyd

My Daily Workout   Date.   /   /

I notice a fear that

* ....[Breathe it out]
* ....[Breathe it out]
* ....[Breathe it out]
* ....[Breathe it out]
* ....[Breathe it out]

I notice these judgments about others

* ....[Breathe it out]
* ....[Breathe it out]

Two things I'm accepting & affirming about myself

* ....
* ....

One Way in which I've been playing the martyr

* ....[Breathe it out]

In reality I am: ....

Today I feel obliged to

* ....[Breathe it out]

My work-around: ....
* ....[Breathe it out]

My work-around: ....

Today I Need [for me]

* ....

My work-around: ....
* ....

My work-around: ....
* ....

My work-around: ....

[Use the extension pages at the back of this workbook if you need to do more]

(c) Wren Síofra Lloyd

My Daily Workout   Date.   /   /

I notice a fear that

* ....[Breathe it out]
* ....[Breathe it out]
* ....[Breathe it out]
* ....[Breathe it out]
* ....[Breathe it out]

I notice these judgments about others

* ....[Breathe it out]
* ....[Breathe it out]

Two things I'm accepting & affirming about myself

* ....
* ....

One Way in which I've been playing the martyr

* ....[Breathe it out]

In reality I am: ....

Today I feel obliged to

* ....[Breathe it out]

My work-around: ....
* ....[Breathe it out]

My work-around: ....

Today I Need [for me]

* ....

My work-around: ....
* ....

My work-around: ....
* ....

My work-around: ....

[Use the extension pages at the back of this workbook if you need to do more]

(c) Wren Síofra Lloyd

My Daily Workout   Date.   /   /

I notice a fear that

* ....[Breathe it out]
* ....[Breathe it out]
* ....[Breathe it out]
* ....[Breathe it out]
* ....[Breathe it out]

I notice these judgments about others

* ....[Breathe it out]
* ....[Breathe it out]

Two things I'm accepting & affirming about myself

* ....
* ....

One Way in which I've been playing the martyr

* ....[Breathe it out]

In reality I am: ....

Today I feel obliged to

* ....[Breathe it out]

My work-around: ....
* ....[Breathe it out]

My work-around: ....

Today I Need [for me]

* ....

My work-around: ....
* ....

My work-around: ....
* ....

My work-around: ....

[Use the extension pages at the back of this workbook if you need to do more]

(c) Wren Síofra Lloyd

My Daily Workout   Date.   /   /

I notice a fear that

* ....[Breathe it out]
* ....[Breathe it out]
* ....[Breathe it out]
* ....[Breathe it out]
* ....[Breathe it out]

I notice these judgments about others

* ....[Breathe it out]
* ....[Breathe it out]

Two things I'm accepting & affirming about myself

* ....
* ....

One Way in which I've been playing the martyr

* ....[Breathe it out]
In reality I am: ....

Today I feel obliged to

* ....[Breathe it out]
My work-around: ....
* ....[Breathe it out]
My work-around: ....

Today I Need [for me]

* ....
My work-around: ....
* ....
My work-around: ....
* ....
My work-around: ....

[Use the extension pages at the back of this workbook if you need to do more]

(c) Wren Síofra Lloyd

My Week

To Discover Value We Must Evaluate

"In order to love who
you are, you cannot
hate the experiences
that shaped you."
~ Andrea Dykstra

This week's anxiety score: out of 10 =

How does it compare to last week?

This week's 'shame' score: out of 10 =

How does to compare to last week?

What challenges did you overcome?

Did you begin to see any surprising changes?

(c) Wren Síofra Lloyd

My Daily Workout   Date.   /   /

I notice a fear that

* ....[Breathe it out]
* ....[Breathe it out]
* ....[Breathe it out]
* ....[Breathe it out]
* ....[Breathe it out]

I notice these judgments about others

* ....[Breathe it out]
* ....[Breathe it out]

Two things I'm accepting & affirming about myself

* ....
* ....

One Way in which I've been playing the martyr

* ....[Breathe it out]

In reality I am: ....

Today I feel obliged to

* ....[Breathe it out]

My work-around: ....
* ....[Breathe it out]

My work-around: ....

Today I Need [for me]

* ....

My work-around: ....
* ....

My work-around: ....
* ....

My work-around: ....

[Use the extension pages at the back of this workbook if you need to do more]

(c) Wren Síofra Lloyd

My Daily Workout   Date.   /   /

I notice a fear that

* ....[Breathe it out]
* ....[Breathe it out]
* ....[Breathe it out]
* ....[Breathe it out]
* ....[Breathe it out]

I notice these judgments about others

* ....[Breathe it out]
* ....[Breathe it out]

Two things I'm accepting & affirming about myself

*
....
*
....

One Way in which I've been playing the martyr

* ....[Breathe it out]

In reality I am: ....

Today I feel obliged to

* ....[Breathe it out]

My work-around: ....
* ....[Breathe it out]

My work-around: ....

Today I Need [for me]

*
....

My work-around: ....
*
....

My work-around: ....
*
....

My work-around: ....

[Use the extension pages at the back of this workbook if you need to do more]

(c) Wren Síofra Lloyd

My Daily Workout   Date.   /   /

I notice a fear that
* ....[Breathe it out]
* ....[Breathe it out]
* ....[Breathe it out]
* ....[Breathe it out]
* ....[Breathe it out]

I notice these judgments about others
* ....[Breathe it out]
* ....[Breathe it out]

Two things I'm accepting & affirming about myself
*
....
*
....

One Way in which I've been playing the martyr
* ....[Breathe it out]

In reality I am: ....

Today I feel obliged to
* ....[Breathe it out]

My work-around: ....
* ....[Breathe it out]

My work-around: ....

Today I Need [for me]
*
....

My work-around: ....
*
....

My work-around: ....
*
....

My work-around: ....

[Use the extension pages at the back of this workbook if you need to do more]

(c) Wren Síofra Lloyd

My Daily Workout   Date.   /   /

I notice a fear that

* ....[Breathe it out]
* ....[Breathe it out]
* ....[Breathe it out]
* ....[Breathe it out]
* ....[Breathe it out]

I notice these judgments about others

* ....[Breathe it out]
* ....[Breathe it out]

Two things I'm accepting & affirming about myself

* ....
* ....

One Way in which I've been playing the martyr

* ....[Breathe it out]

In reality I am: ....

Today I feel obliged to

* ....[Breathe it out]

My work-around: ....
* ....[Breathe it out]

My work-around: ....

Today I Need [for me]

* ....

My work-around: ....
* ....

My work-around: ....
* ....

My work-around: ....

[Use the extension pages at the back of this workbook if you need to do more]

(c) Wren Síofra Lloyd

My Daily Workout   Date.   /   /

I notice a fear that

* ....[Breathe it out]
* ....[Breathe it out]
* ....[Breathe it out]
* ....[Breathe it out]
* ....[Breathe it out]

I notice these judgments about others

* ....[Breathe it out]
* ....[Breathe it out]

Two things I'm accepting & affirming about myself

* ....
* ....

One Way in which I've been playing the martyr

* ....[Breathe it out]

In reality I am: ....

Today I feel obliged to

* ....[Breathe it out]

My work-around: ....

* ....[Breathe it out]

My work-around: ....

Today I Need [for me]

* ....

My work-around: ....

* ....

My work-around: ....

* ....

My work-around: ....

[Use the extension pages at the back of this workbook if you need to do more]

(c) Wren Síofra Lloyd

My Daily Workout   Date. / /

I notice a fear that

* ....[Breathe it out]
* ....[Breathe it out]
* ....[Breathe it out]
* ....[Breathe it out]
* ....[Breathe it out]

I notice these judgments about others

* ....[Breathe it out]
* ....[Breathe it out]

Two things I'm accepting & affirming about myself

* ....
* ....

One Way in which I've been playing the martyr

* ....[Breathe it out]

In reality I am: ....

Today I feel obliged to

* ....[Breathe it out]

My work-around: ....
* ....[Breathe it out]

My work-around: ....

Today I Need [for me]

* ....

My work-around: ....
* ....

My work-around: ....
* ....

My work-around: ....

[Use the extension pages at the back of this workbook if you need to do more]

(c) Wren Síofra Lloyd

My Daily Workout   Date.   /   /

I notice a fear that
* ....[Breathe it out]
* ....[Breathe it out]
* ....[Breathe it out]
* ....[Breathe it out]
* ....[Breathe it out]

I notice these judgments about others
* ....[Breathe it out]
* ....[Breathe it out]

Two things I'm accepting & affirming about myself
* ....
* ....

One Way in which I've been playing the martyr
* ....[Breathe it out]

In reality I am: ....

Today I feel obliged to
* ....[Breathe it out]

My work-around: ....
* ....[Breathe it out]

My work-around: ....

Today I Need [for me]
* ....

My work-around: ....
* ....

My work-around: ....
* ....

My work-around: ....

[Use the extension pages at the back of this workbook if you need to do more]

(c) Wren Síofra Lloyd

My Week

To Discover Value We Must Evaluate

"Beauty begins the moment
you decide to be yourself."
~ Coco Chanel

This week's anxiety score: out of 10 =

How does it compare to last week?

This week's 'shame' score: out of 10 =

How does to compare to last week?

What challenges did you overcome?

Did you begin to see any surprising changes?

(c) Wren Síofra Lloyd

My Daily Workout   Date.   /   /

I notice a fear that
* ....[Breathe it out]
* ....[Breathe it out]
* ....[Breathe it out]
* ....[Breathe it out]
* ....[Breathe it out]

I notice these judgments about others
* ....[Breathe it out]
* ....[Breathe it out]

Two things I'm accepting & affirming about myself
*
....
*
....

One Way in which I've been playing the martyr
* ....[Breathe it out]
In reality I am: ....

Today I feel obliged to
* ....[Breathe it out]
My work-around: ....
* ....[Breathe it out]
My work-around: ....

Today I Need [for me]
*
....
My work-around: ....
*
....
My work-around: ....
*
....
My work-around: ....

[Use the extension pages at the back of this workbook if you need to do more]

(c) Wren Síofra Lloyd

My Daily Workout   Date.   /   /

I notice a fear that
* ....[Breathe it out]
* ....[Breathe it out]
* ....[Breathe it out]
* ....[Breathe it out]
* ....[Breathe it out]

I notice these judgments about others
* ....[Breathe it out]
* ....[Breathe it out]

Two things I'm accepting & affirming about myself
* ....
* ....

One Way in which I've been playing the martyr
* ....[Breathe it out]
In reality I am: ....

Today I feel obliged to
* ....[Breathe it out]
My work-around: ....
* ....[Breathe it out]
My work-around: ....

Today I Need [for me]
* ....
My work-around: ....
* ....
My work-around: ....
* ....
My work-around: ....

[Use the extension pages at the back of this workbook if you need to do more]

(c) Wren Síofra Lloyd

My Daily Workout

Date. / /

I notice a fear that

* ....[Breathe it out]
* ....[Breathe it out]
* ....[Breathe it out]
* ....[Breathe it out]
* ....[Breathe it out]

I notice these judgments about others

* ....[Breathe it out]
* ....[Breathe it out]

Two things I'm accepting & affirming about myself

* ....
* ....

One Way in which I've been playing the martyr

* ....[Breathe it out]

In reality I am: ....

Today I feel obliged to

* ....[Breathe it out]

My work-around: ....
* ....[Breathe it out]

My work-around: ....

Today I Need [for me]

* ....

My work-around: ....
* ....

My work-around: ....
* ....

My work-around: ....

[Use the extension pages at the back of this workbook if you need to do more]

(c) Wren Síofra Lloyd

My Daily Workout   Date.   /   /

I notice a fear that
* ....[Breathe it out]
* ....[Breathe it out]
* ....[Breathe it out]
* ....[Breathe it out]
* ....[Breathe it out]

I notice these judgments about others
* ....[Breathe it out]
* ....[Breathe it out]

Two things I'm accepting & affirming about myself
*
....
*
....

One Way in which I've been playing the martyr
* ....[Breathe it out]
In reality I am: ....

Today I feel obliged to
* ....[Breathe it out]
My work-around: ....
* ....[Breathe it out]
My work-around: ....

Today I Need [for me]
*
....
My work-around: ....
*
....
My work-around: ....
*
....
My work-around: ....

[Use the extension pages at the back of this workbook if you need to do more]

(c) Wren Síofra Lloyd

My Daily Workout   Date.   /   /

I notice a fear that

* ....[Breathe it out]
* ....[Breathe it out]
* ....[Breathe it out]
* ....[Breathe it out]
* ....[Breathe it out]

I notice these judgments about others

* ....[Breathe it out]
* ....[Breathe it out]

Two things I'm accepting & affirming about myself

* ....
* ....

One Way in which I've been playing the martyr

* ....[Breathe it out]
In reality I am: ....

Today I feel obliged to

* ....[Breathe it out]
My work-around: ....
* ....[Breathe it out]
My work-around: ....

Today I Need [for me]

* ....
My work-around: ....
* ....
My work-around: ....
* ....
My work-around: ....

[Use the extension pages at the back of this workbook if you need to do more]

(c) Wren Síofra Lloyd

My Daily Workout   Date.   /   /

I notice a fear that
* ....[Breathe it out]
* ....[Breathe it out]
* ....[Breathe it out]
* ....[Breathe it out]
* ....[Breathe it out]

I notice these judgments about others
* ....[Breathe it out]
* ....[Breathe it out]

Two things I'm accepting & affirming about myself
* ....
* ....

One Way in which I've been playing the martyr
* ....[Breathe it out]
In reality I am: ....

Today I feel obliged to
* ....[Breathe it out]
My work-around: ....
* ....[Breathe it out]
My work-around: ....

Today I Need [for me]
* ....
My work-around: ....
* ....
My work-around: ....
* ....
My work-around: ....

[Use the extension pages at the back of this workbook if you need to do more]

(c) Wren Síofra Lloyd

My Daily Workout

Date.   /   /

I notice a fear that

* ....[Breathe it out]
* ....[Breathe it out]
* ....[Breathe it out]
* ....[Breathe it out]
* ....[Breathe it out]

I notice these judgments about others

* ....[Breathe it out]
* ....[Breathe it out]

Two things I'm accepting & affirming about myself

* ....
* ....

One Way in which I've been playing the martyr

* ....[Breathe it out]

In reality I am: ....

Today I feel obliged to

* ....[Breathe it out]

My work-around: ....

* ....[Breathe it out]

My work-around: ....

Today I Need [for me]

* ....

My work-around: ....

* ....

My work-around: ....

* ....

My work-around: ....

[Use the extension pages at the back of this workbook if you need to do more]

(c) Wren Síofra Lloyd

My Week

To Discover Value We Must Evaluate

"You find peace not by
rearranging the circumstances
of your life, but by realizing
who you are at the
deepest level."
~ Eckhart Tolle

This week's anxiety score: out of 10 =

How does it compare to last week?

This week's 'shame' score: out of 10 =

How does to compare to last week?

What challenges did you overcome?

Did you begin to see any surprising changes?

(c) Wren Síofra Lloyd

Completion

To Discover Value We Must Evaluate

What 2 or more important things did you learned about yourself?

What was the most important change that happened to you?

What ways have you come to set better boundaries?

What ways have you found to meet your needs?

Which judgments and fears have you let go of?

(c) Wren Síofra Lloyd

Completion Continued

What more do you want to celebrate & remember? [Draw or write!]

(c) Wren Síofra Lloyd

MORE FEARS
Don't forget to breathe them out

(c) Wren Síofra Lloyd

MORE FEARS
Don't forget to breathe them out

(c) Wren Síofra Lloyd

MORE JUDGMENTS
Don't forget to breathe them out

(c) Wren Síofra Lloyd

MORE JUDGMENTS

Don't forget to breathe them out

(c) Wren Síofra Lloyd

MORE AFFIRMATIONS

(c) Wren Síofra Lloyd

MORE AFFIRMATIONS

(c) Wren Síofra Lloyd

MORE MARTYRDOM (& "REALLY I AM")

(c) Wren Síofra Lloyd

MORE MARTYRDOM (&"REALLY I AM")

(c) Wren Síofra Lloyd

MORE OBLIGATIONS & WORKAROUNDS

Don't forget to breathe them out

(c) Wren Síofra Lloyd

MORE OBLIGATIONS & WORKAROUNDS

Don't forget to breathe them out

(c) Wren Síofra Lloyd

MORE NEEDS & WORKAROUNDS

(c) Wren Síofra Lloyd

MORE NEEDS & WORKAROUNDS

(c) Wren Síofra Lloyd

Notes

(c) Wren Síofra Lloyd

Notes

(c) Wren Síofra Lloyd

Notes

(c) Wren Síofra Lloyd

Notes

(c) Wren Síofra Lloyd

Printed in Great Britain
by Amazon